# abc English

# Phonics

## Level 4

abc English Phonics, Level 4
Systematic Phonics Lessons for Adult & Adolescent English Language Learners

Copyright 2023, abc English
abceng.org
Jennifer Christenson

R230517

ISBN 979-8-88702-005-1

Image licensing: istock.com

# Contents

Teachers:
Slideshow lessons to accompany this book
can be found at abceng.org/library.

# Regular Verbs 1

| | | |
|---|---|---|
| clean | use | call |
| cleans | uses | calls |
| cleaning | using | calling |
| cleaned | used | called |
| will clean | will use | will call |
| going to clean | going to use | going to call |

| | | |
|---|---|---|
| stay | move | change |
| stays | moves | changes |
| staying | moving | changing |
| stayed | moved | changed |
| will stay | will move | will change |
| going to stay | going to move | going to change |

|  |  |  |  |
|---|---|---|---|
| clean | stay | change | call |

# Sentences

1.  They call me every week.

2.  She cleans her house every Saturday.

3.  My son is using the computer right now.

4.  They are going to move to a different city next month.

5.  He will change schools next year.

6.  She stayed home from work yesterday because she was sick.

# Regular Verbs 2

| | | |
|---|---|---|
| look | work | ask |
| looks | works | asks |
| looking | working | asking |
| looked | worked | asked |
| will look | will work | will ask |
| going to look | going to work | going to ask |

| | | |
|---|---|---|
| help | wash | fix |
| helps | washes | fixes |
| helping | washing | fixing |
| helped | washed | fixed |
| will help | will wash | will fix |
| going to help | going to wash | going to fix |

|  |  |  | 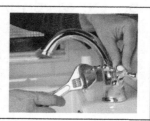 |
|---|---|---|---|
| look | ask | help | fix |

# Sentences

1. She is looking for a new job.

2. I worked overtime yesterday. I worked 12 hours!

3. Tomorrow I will ask my supervisor if I can have a day off.

4. My neighbor helps me a lot. She helps me every week.

5. He fixed my sink last week. It was broken, but now it is fine.

6. They wash the dishes every evening after we eat.

# Regular Verbs 3

| | | |
|---|---|---|
| wait | visit | taste |
| waits | visits | tastes |
| waiting | visiting | tasting |
| waited | visited | tasted |
| will wait | will visit | will taste |
| going to wait | going to visit | going to taste |

| | | |
|---|---|---|
| start | end | decide |
| starts | ends | decides |
| starting | ending | deciding |
| started | ended | decided |
| will start | will end | will decide |
| going to start | going to end | going to decide |

|  |  |  |  |
|---|---|---|---|
| wait | visit | taste | decide |

# Sentences

1.  The class starts at 6:30 and ends at 8:30.

2.  She is tasting the food. It tastes good!

3.  They decided to move to a different apartment.

4.  They are waiting in a long line at the bank.

5.  She is going to visit her sister next Saturday.

6.  He started a new job yesterday. He likes it!

# Pronunciation of -es

| /s/ | /uz/ |
|---|---|
| clean - cleans | use - uses |
| call - calls | kiss - kisses |
| stay - stays | dance - dances |
| move - moves | practice - practices |
| look - looks | fix - fixes |
| work - works | relax - relaxes |
| ask - asks | wash - washes |
| help - helps | finish - finishes |
| wait - waits | teach - teaches |
| visit - visits | watch - watches |
| start - starts | change - changes |

|  |  |  |  |
|---|---|---|---|
| kisses | dances | relaxes | teaches |

## Sentences

1.  She teaches preschool. She likes her job a lot.

2.  He washes the dishes every evening. His son helps.

3.  She practices with the team every day after school.

4.  Who changes the baby's diaper? Sometimes me. Sometimes my husband. Sometimes my older kids.

5.  After she finishes her work, she helps her friends.

6.  They love to dance. He dances with his kids every weekend.

# My Day

Usually, I wake up at 5:30. I take a shower and get dressed. Then I drink coffee and eat breakfast. I wake up my daughter and make food for her. I go to the bus stop at 6:30. I take the bus to work and arrive at 7:15. I start work at 7:30.

I am busy at work. I don't have much time to sit down. I have a break at 9:30 and I eat lunch at 12:00. I finish work at 3:30, then I take the bus back home.

After work, I go home and rest a little. Then I make dinner and eat with my daughter. After we eat, sometimes I go outside to walk. Sometimes I relax and watch TV. Sometimes I talk on the phone. I get ready for bed around 9:00 and I usually go to sleep around 10:00.

# My Daughter's Day

My daughter is fourteen years old. She is in high school. She wakes up at 6:15. She takes a shower and gets dressed. Then she eats breakfast and drinks juice. She takes the bus to school. The bus comes at 6:45. She arrives at school at 7:15. School starts at 7:30.

She is very busy at school. She goes to class and talks with friends. She eats lunch at 11:30. She finishes class at 2:30. She is on the track team, so after school she practices with the team. She comes home around 4:00.

At home, she rests a little. Then she helps me make dinner. After we eat, she does her homework or watches TV. She gets ready for bed around 9:00 and she usually goes to sleep around 10:00.

# Pronunciation of -ed

| /ud/ | /t/ | /d/ |
|:---:|:---:|:---:|
| ended | looked | cleaned |
| decided | worked | used |
| waited | asked | called |
| visited | helped | stayed |
| tasted | washed | moved |
| started | fixed | changed |
| | | |
| folded | passed | showed |
| planted | talked | played |
| deleted | cooked | opened |

folded

planted

talked

opened

# Sentences

1. They played basketball last Saturday.

2. I deleted the message.

3. I talked to my friend last week.

4. We cooked a lot of food for the holiday.

5. He planted tomatoes in his garden.

6. She passed the driver license test.

# Verbs with Final -y

| | | |
|---|---|---|
| study | carry | worry |
| studies | carries | worries |
| studying | carrying | worrying |
| studied | carried | worried |
| will study | will carry | will worry |
| going to study | going to carry | going to worry |

| | | |
|---|---|---|
| try | cry | apply |
| tries | cries | applies |
| trying | crying | applying |
| tried | cried | applied |
| will try | will cry | will apply |
| going to try | going to cry | going to apply |

|  |  |  |  |
|---|---|---|---|
| study | carry | worry | try |

## Sentences

1. My baby cried for a long time last night. I'm very tired now!

2. She studies English every day. She really wants to learn.

3. We need to carry this sofa upstairs. Can you help us?

4. They are worried about money. They have a lot of problems right now.

5. I applied for a new job yesterday. I hope I get an interview.

6. Our little girl is trying to walk. She can almost walk by herself.

# Verb Spelling Rules

## 1. Change -y to i
If a verb ends in -y, change y to i before -es or -ed.

| | |
|---|---|
| study - studies - studied | try - tries - tried |
| carry - carries - carried | cry - cries - cried |
| worry - worries - worried | apply - applies - applied |

## 2. Add -es
If a verb ends in s, ch, sh, x, or o, add -es.

| | | |
|---|---|---|
| kiss - kisses | watch - watches | relax - relaxes |
| wash - washes | mix - mixes | go - goes |
| brush - brushes | fix - fixes | do - does |

|  |  |  |  |
|---|---|---|---|
| brush | mix | do | kiss |

## Sentences

1.  She washes her face and brushes her teeth before bed.

2.  Every day after class, she goes home and does her homework. She studies a lot.

3.  She is making a cake. First, she gets flour, sugar, and cocoa and mixes it together. What's next?

4.  In the evening, he watches TV and relaxes.

5.  Every day at school, she reads, writes, and uses the computer.

6.  He fixes things every day. Right now, he is fixing a light.

# More Verb Spelling Rules

## 3. Drop -e
If a verb ends in -e, drop the -e before -ing.

| | | |
|---|---|---|
| drive - driving | write - writing | come - coming |
| move - moving | ride - riding | make - making |
| dance - dancing | use - using | give - giving |

## 4. Doubling
If you see 1 vowel and 1 letter after,
use double letters before -ing or -ed.

| | | |
|---|---|---|
| sit - sitting | clap - clapped | shop - shopping |
| run - running | stop - stopped | swim - swimming |
| jog - jogging | drip - dripped | begin - beginning |

| ride | make | jog | drip |
|---|---|---|---|

## Sentences

1.  They are laughing and dancing.

2.  My bathroom sink is dripping. Can you come fix it?

3.  She is riding a bicycle. He is riding a motorcycle.

4.  She is making bread. She makes it in an oven outside.

5.  Every Saturday in the park, I see people walking, jogging, and running.

6.  I'm in a beginning level English class. We practice reading and writing every day.

# Irregular Verbs 1

| | | |
|---|---|---|
| go | come | give |
| goes | comes | gives |
| going | coming | giving |
| went | came | gave |
| will go | will come | will give |
| going to go | going to come | going to give |

| | | |
|---|---|---|
| meet | lose | find |
| meets | loses | finds |
| meeting | losing | finding |
| met | lost | found |
| will meet | will lose | will find |
| going to meet | going to lose | going to find |

|  |  |  |  |
|---|---|---|---|
| go - went | give - gave | meet - met | lose - lost |

## Sentences

1. Did you lose your phone?
      Yes, I lost it.

2. Did you find your wallet?
      Yes, I found it!

3. When did you meet with his teacher?
      I met with her last week.

4. Did you give him the gift?
      Yes, I gave it to him yesterday.

5. Did they come to your house?
      Yes, they came on Sunday.

6. When did you go to the bank?
      I went to the bank last Friday.

# Irregular Verbs 2

| | | |
|---|---|---|
| get | forget | fall |
| gets | forgets | falls |
| getting | forgetting | falling |
| got | forgot | fell |
| will get | will forget | will fall |
| going to get | going to forget | going to fall |

| | | |
|---|---|---|
| know | grow | fly |
| knows | grows | flies |
| knowing | growing | flying |
| knew | grew | flew |
| will know | will grow | will fly |
| going to know | going to grow | going to fly |

|  |  |  |  |
|---|---|---|---|
| get - got | fall - fell | grow - grew | fly - flew |

## Sentences

1.  Did you forget about the appointment?
    Yes. Sorry, I forgot.

2.  Did you get the job?
    Yes, I got it!

3.  Where did she fall?
    She fell on the stairs.

4.  Did you fly when you went to visit?
    Yes, I flew.

5.  Did you know the answer?
    Yes, I knew it.

6.  Where did you grow up?
    I grew up in New York.

# Irregular Verbs 3

| | | |
|---|---|---|
| say | tell | make |
| says | tells | makes |
| saying | telling | making |
| said | told | made |
| will say | will tell | will make |
| going to say | going to tell | going to make |

| | | |
|---|---|---|
| think | buy | bring |
| thinks | buys | brings |
| thinking | buying | bringing |
| thought | bought | brought |
| will think | will buy | will bring |
| going to think | going to buy | going to bring |

|  |  |  |  |
|---|---|---|---|
| say - said | tell - told | make - made | buy - bought |

# Sentences

1. What did they say?
   > They said I can come for an interview.

2. When did they tell you to come?
   > They told me to come at 3:00.

3. Did you make these samosas?
   > Yes! I made them last night.

4. Did you bring your ID?
   > Yes, I brought it. Here it is.

5. Did you buy milk?
   > Yes, I bought milk, and I also bought bananas and rice.

6. Do you think you will get a car?
   > I thought about it, but now I think I will wait.

# Irregular Verbs 4

| | | |
|---|---|---|
| sleep | keep | spend |
| sleeps | keeps | spends |
| sleeping | keeping | spending |
| slept | kept | spent |
| will sleep | will keep | will spend |
| going to sleep | going to keep | going to spend |

| | | |
|---|---|---|
| leave | hear | read |
| leaves | hears | reads |
| leaving | hearing | reading |
| left | heard | read |
| will leave | will hear | will read |
| going to leave | going to hear | going to read |

|  |  |  |  |
|---|---|---|---|
| sleep - slept | leave - left | hear - heard | read - read |

## Sentences

1. Did you keep the receipt?
   Yes, I kept it. I have it here.

2. How many hours did you sleep last night?
   I only slept three hours. I'm really tired.

3. How much did you spend on your new phone?
   I spent $350. Phones are expensive!

4. What time did you leave work yesterday?
   I left at 3:30.

5. Did you hear the fire truck?
   Yes, I heard it.

6. Did you read the letter?
   Yes, I read it.

# Next Weekend

Next weekend, I am going to be very busy. On Saturday, I will clean the house and I will do the laundry. Then I will go shopping. I am going to make a lot of food. In the evening, my family is going to come over to my house. We will eat a lot of good food.

On Sunday, I am going to go to a party at my friend's house. She is pregnant. We are going to give her gifts for the new baby. In the morning, I will buy a gift for her. The party is going to be in the afternoon. I will bring a cake for everyone to eat. After the party, I will come home and relax. If I have time, I will study English a little. Then I will get ready for Monday and go to bed. I will sleep well!

# Last Weekend

Last weekend, I was very busy. On Saturday, I cleaned the house and I did the laundry. Then I went shopping. I made a lot of food. In the evening, my family came over to my house. We ate a lot of good food.

On Sunday, I went to a party at my friend's house. She is pregnant. We gave her gifts for the new baby. In the morning, I bought a gift for her. The party was in the afternoon. I brought a cake for everyone to eat. After the party, I came home and relaxed. I had some time, so I studied English a little. Then I got ready for Monday and went to bed. I slept well!

## Perfect Tense

| | | |
|---|---|---|
| live | do | see |
| lives | does | sees |
| living | doing | seeing |
| lived | did | saw |
| will live | will do | will see |
| going to live | going to do | going to see |
| have lived | have done | have seen |

| | | |
|---|---|---|
| take | ride | break |
| takes | rides | breaks |
| taking | riding | breaking |
| took | rode | broke |
| will take | will ride | will break |
| going to take | going to ride | going to break |
| have taken | have ridden | have broken |

|  |  |  |  |
|---|---|---|---|
| have seen | have taken | have ridden | have broken |

## Sentences

1. How long have you lived here?
   > I have lived here for two and a half years.

2. Have you done this kind of work before?
   > No, I have never done this before. Can you show me?

3. How long have you taken English classes here?
   > I have taken classes here for six months.

4. Have you seen my son? I don't know where he is.
   > No, sorry. I have not seen him.

5. Have you ridden a motorcycle before?
   > No, I have never ridden a motorcycle.

6. Have you ever broken your phone screen?
   > Yes, I have broken my screen two times!

# Nouns: Singular and Plural

| | |
|---|---|
| girl - girls<br>boy - boys<br>student - students<br>teacher - teachers | banana - bananas<br>carrot - carrots<br>cucumber - cucumbers<br>onion - onions |
| friend - friends<br>brother - brothers<br>sister - sisters<br>cousin - cousins | fork - forks<br>spoon - spoons<br>bowl - bowls<br>pan - pans |
| house - houses<br>school - schools<br>lake - lakes<br>mountain - mountains | day - days<br>month - months<br>year - years<br>minute - minutes |

|  |  |  |  |
|---|---|---|---|
| pans | bowls | cucumbers | mountains |

## Sentences

1. Do you have any brothers or sisters?

2. She met some good friends at school.

3. There are a lot of students in this class, and only one teacher.

4. They have two kids. One is four years old, and the other is six months old.

5. Please wait. The doctor will be with you in ten minutes.

6. Are there any mountains near your city?

# Plural Noun Spelling Rules

## 1. Add -es

If a noun ends in s, ch, sh, x or o, add -es.

| | | |
|---|---|---|
| dress - dresses | peach - peaches | box - boxes |
| class - classes | inch - inches | tomato - tomatoes |
| glass - glasses | dish - dishes | potato - potatoes |

## 2. Change -y to i

If a noun ends in -y, change y to i and add -es.

| | | |
|---|---|---|
| baby - babies | cherry - cherries | city - cities |
| lady - ladies | berry - berries | country - countries |

## 3. Change f to v

If a noun ends in -f or -fe, change f to v and add -es.

| | | |
|---|---|---|
| knife - knives | leaf - leaves | scarf - scarves |
| life - lives | half - halves | wolf - wolves |

| peaches | cherries | berries | scarves |
|---|---|---|---|

34

# Sentences

1. She is five feet, five inches tall. That's the same as 165 centimeters.

2. He needs glasses. Glasses help him see things better.

3. Wolves are animals that live in mountains and forests.

4. Do the leaves change colors in your area?

5. I need to get some forks, knives, and spoons for my kitchen.

6. He knows how to grow things. He grows tomatoes, carrots, beans, potatoes, and a lot more.

# Regular Plural Nouns
(Add -s)

| | |
|---|---|
| pencil - pencils<br>book - books<br>paper - papers | door - doors<br>window - windows<br>light - lights |

# Irregular Plural Nouns
(Don't add -s)

| | |
|---|---|
| man - men<br>woman - women<br>child - children<br>person - people<br><br>foot - feet<br>tooth - teeth | mouse - mice<br>goose - geese<br><br>sheep - sheep<br>fish - fish<br>deer - deer<br>moose - moose |

|  |  |  |  |
|---|---|---|---|
| goose | sheep | moose | deer |

## Sentences

1. My brother has one child. My sister has two children.

2. There are seven women and eight men in this group.

3. One person is speaking. The other people are listening.

4. A mouse is a small animal. I don't like mice in my house.

5. A goose is a large bird. A group of geese will fly in a V shape.

6. A moose is a very large animal. There are a lot of moose in Canada.

# Contractions

$$I + am = I'm$$

$$is + not = isn't$$

$$should + have = should've$$

$$I + would = I'd$$

$$he + will = he'll$$

$$will + not = won't$$

| I'm | isn't | can't | I'll | I've |
|---|---|---|---|---|
| he's | aren't | won't | he'll | they've |
| she's | wasn't | couldn't | she'll | could've |
| you're | weren't | shouldn't | they'll | should've |
| they're | don't | wouldn't | I'd | would've |
| we're | doesn't | haven't | he'd | what's |
| it's | didn't | hasn't | she'd | where's |

| | | |
|---|---|---|
|  |  |  |
| You're welcome. | She isn't happy. | I couldn't see. |

## Sentences

1.  It's raining. I should've brought an umbrella.

2.  He's tired. He didn't sleep much last night.

3.  I could've helped you, but I wasn't home.

4.  Sorry, I won't be able to come tomorrow. I'm busy.

5.  They've lived here for two years. They're happy here.

6.  She can't speak much English. She'd like to learn more.

## Apostrophe + s

| | |
|---|---|
| the teacher's phone | the phone of the teacher |
| the school's name | the name of the school |
| the manager's office | the office of the manager |

| | |
|---|---|
| my father's father | the father of my father |
| my uncle's daughter | the daughter of my uncle |
| my friend's brother | the brother of my friend |

| | |
|---|---|
| Sam's laptop | the laptop of Sam |
| Alisha's car | the car of Alisha |
| Jessica's bag | the bag of Jessica |

|  |  |  |
|---|---|---|
| Sam's laptop | Alisha's car | Jessica's bag |

## Sentences

1. My mother's mother is my grandmother.

2. My brother's son is my nephew.

3. My friend's husband's brother lives in New York City.

4. Is that your laptop? No, it's my sister's laptop.

5. Is that your car? No, it's my neighbor's car.

6. Can you take this to the supervisor's office? Sure!

# The Earth

Earth is the name of the planet that we live on. It is a giant blue sphere that moves around the sun.

There are eight planets that move around the sun. Earth is the third planet from the sun. Earth is unique because most of its surface is covered by water. Earth is the only planet where people can live. It is the only planet that has enough water and oxygen to support life. It is also a good temperature for people to live. Other planets are much too hot or too cold.

It takes 365 days for the earth to revolve around the sun one time. One revolution is called a year. It takes 24 hours for the earth to rotate around its axis one time. One rotation is called a day.

The sun shines on half of the earth at a time. The other half of the earth is facing away from the sun. It is always day on one side of the earth, and night on the other side.

It looks like the sun is moving around the earth. However, the sun is not moving. The earth is rotating.

# The Moon

When you look up in the night sky, sometimes you see the moon, and sometimes you don't. Sometimes it is big and round, and sometimes it is a thin crescent. Why?

The moon looks like a bright light in the night sky. However, the moon doesn't make light by itself. The moon reflects light from the sun. The light from the moon is really light reflected from the sun.

A full moon is visible when the earth is between the moon and the sun. The moon reflects light from the sun, and people on earth see a full moon. A new moon occurs two weeks later when the moon is on the other side of the earth. The moon reflects light from the sun, but you can't see the light because it is shining away from the earth.

The surface of the moon is dry and dusty. There is no water. There is no oxygen. Astronauts visited the moon for the first time in 1969. It took four days to fly there. They had to wear space suits. They got oxygen from the space suits. The suits also protected them from the moon's extreme temperatures.

# Suffix -y, -ly

| | |
|---|---|
| dirty | slowly |
| sleepy | quickly |
| rocky | safely |
| sandy | loudly |
| dusty | quietly |
| rusty | completely |
| messy | carefully |
| healthy | dangerously |
| wealthy | finally |
| noisy | exactly |
| windy | regularly |
| rainy | absolutely |

| sandy | rusty | noisy | wealthy |
|---|---|---|---|

# Sentences

1. It is important to drive carefully.

2. My phone battery is completely dead. I need to charge it.

3. They exercise regularly. They walk four or five times per week.

4. Do you usually speak loudly or quietly?

5. Do you eat lunch quickly or slowly?

6. "Early to bed and early to rise, makes a man healthy, wealthy, and wise."

# Suffix -less, -ful, -able

| | | |
|---|---|---|
| painless | helpful | breakable |
| wireless | colorful | comfortable |
| toothless | stressful | enjoyable |
| speechless | careful | available |
| tasteless | grateful | adorable |
| fearless | cheerful | understandable |
| jobless | harmful | washable |
| homeless | successful | disposable |
| breathless | beautiful | affordable |

| colorful | harmful | comfortable | adorable |
|---|---|---|---|

## Sentences

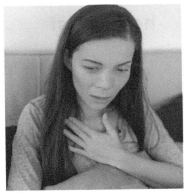  

1. Are you available tomorrow at 11:00?

2. Be careful. It's breakable.

3. She's a successful student. She is hard-working and serious.

4. People who have asthma feel breathless sometimes.

5. It's difficult to find affordable housing in this city.

6. Wow, I don't know what to say! I'm speechless.

# Suffix -er, -or, -ist

| | | |
|---|---|---|
| painter | instructor | pharmacist |
| teacher | actor | machinist |
| baker | operator | artist |
| manager | governor | hair stylist |
| lawyer | director | therapist |
| plumber | doctor | dentist |
| server | | |
| bus driver | | |
| police officer | | |

| instructor | actor | machinist | artist |
|---|---|---|---|

# Sentences

1.  What kind of training do you need to be a bus driver or truck driver?

2.  A pharmacist can answer questions about medicine.

3.  A plumber is a person who can fix a sink, shower, or toilet.

4.  We have class three times a week. Our instructor is really good.

5.  My shoulder hurts. I need to visit a physical therapist.

6.  My friend is a hair stylist.

# Suffix -ment, -tion, -ness

| | | |
|---|---|---|
| apartment | instruction | happiness |
| appointment | protection | sadness |
| basement | operation | illness |
| statement | construction | darkness |
| department | infection | kindness |
| punishment | application | weakness |
| pavement | notification | dizziness |
| payment | inspection | business |
| shipment | communication | forgiveness |

| basement | punishment | inspection | forgiveness |
|---|---|---|---|

# Sentences

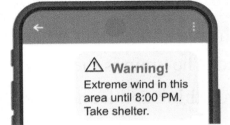

1. Sorry, the shipment is late. It will be here next week.

2. You can check your bank statement online.

3. Germs can cause illness. Washing your hands will help you stay healthy.

4. Take one tablet up to two times a day for dizziness.

5. I got an emergency notification on my phone. It's a warning about the weather.

6. They own a small business. They are busy and successful.

# The Brain

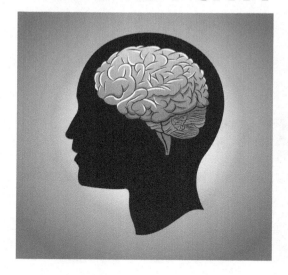

The brain is one of the most important organs in your body. It is located inside your head. The brain is the control center of your body.

The brain is where you think and learn. When you learn something new, you make new connections in the brain. For example, when you learn to read, you make new connections in the brain. When you practice reading more, the connections in the brain will get stronger. If you keep practicing, reading will get easier and faster.

The brain also controls the movement of your body. It sends signals to your body to move your muscles. The brain is connected to the spinal cord and to a network of nerves throughout your body. Your nerves send information back to your brain about things you see, hear, smell, taste, and touch.

It's important to keep your brain safe. Wear a seatbelt in the car. Wear a helmet if you ride a bike. Wear a hard hat if you work in construction. Brain injury is very serious.

# The Heart

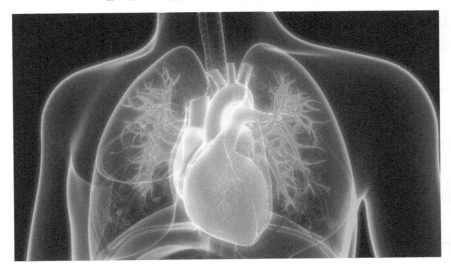

The heart is one of the most important organs in your body. It is located in your chest on the left side. It's about the same size as your fist. The heart is a muscle that pumps blood around your body.

The heart has a left side and a right side. First, the right side of the heart fills up with blood. Then the blood is pumped to the lungs. While the blood is in the lungs, it gets fresh oxygen from the air that you breathe. Next, the blood goes back and fills up the left side of the heart. After that, the blood is pumped out to the rest of your body.

Blood circulates around the body through small tubes called blood vessels. There are two types of blood vessels: arteries and veins. Arteries take blood away from the heart. Veins take blood back to the heart. There is a large artery in your neck where you can feel your pulse. You may be able to see veins in your wrist.

You should do everything you can to keep your heart and lungs healthy. You can exercise, eat healthy food, and avoid smoking. A healthy person has a healthy heart.

# Prefix un-, re-, dis-

| un-<br>(not) | re-<br>(again) | dis-<br>(opposite) |
|:---:|:---:|:---:|
| uncooked | reheat | disagree |
| unhappy | refill | disconnect |
| untied | reset | disappear |
| unlock | remove | disinfect |
| unplug | return | discontinue |
| unload | reuse | dislike |
| unemployed | renew | disability |
| unfurnished | recycle | disrespectful |
| uncomfortable | refund | dishonest |

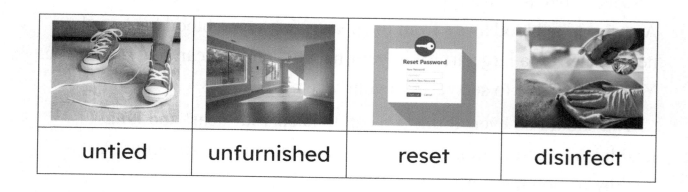

| untied | unfurnished | reset | disinfect |
|:---:|:---:|:---:|:---:|

# Sentences

1. I think it's a good idea for high school students to get an after school job. Do you agree or disagree?

2. My friend is unemployed. He is looking for a job.

3. They always remove their shoes before they go inside.

4. I need to go to the pharmacy to refill my prescription.

5. You need to renew your license every eight years.

6. Before you fix the washing machine, you need to unplug the electricity and disconnect the water.

# Prefix in-, im-, il-, ir-

| **in-** | **im-** | **il-, ir-** |
|:---:|:---:|:---:|
| (not) | (not) | (not) |
| inexpensive | imperfect | illegal |
| incorrect | impatient | illegible |
| incomplete | impossible | |
| inactive | impolite | irregular |
| inedible | immobile | irresponsible |
| informal | improper | |

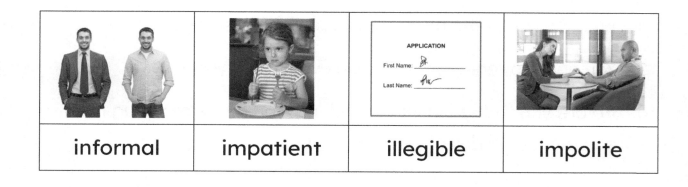

| informal | impatient | illegible | impolite |
|:---:|:---:|:---:|:---:|

# Sentences

1.  Do you know a good place to buy inexpensive clothes for children?

2.  A racoon is an animal that is active at night and inactive during the day.

3.  These berries are inedible.  If you eat them, you'll get sick.

4.  Her job is to check for imperfect tomatoes.

5.  If your baby is not in a car seat, you can get a ticket. It's unsafe and it's illegal.

6.  You need to keep your arm immobile for six weeks.

# Prefix pre-, inter-, super-

| **pre-** (before) | **inter-** (between) | **super-** (over; big) |
|:---:|:---:|:---:|
| preschool | interview | supermarket |
| precooked | international | supervisor |
| prepaid | intersection | superglue |
| pretest | interchange | superman |
| preview | interaction | supersize |
| prefix | intermediate | superintendent |

| precooked | interchange | interaction | superglue |
|:---:|:---:|:---:|:---:|

## Sentences

1. A superintendent is the head of all of the schools in an area.

2. My house is near a busy intersection.

3. First, the students take a pretest to find out what level will be good for them.

4. She has been a preschool teacher for ten years.

5. The International Organization for Migration (IOM) helps people who are moving between countries.

6. A prefix is a word part at the beginning of a word. For example, in the word interview, the prefix inter- means between.

# Prefix trans-, mis-, sub-

| **trans-** (change) | **mis-** (bad) | **sub-** (below) |
|---|---|---|
| translation | misspell | subway |
| transportation | misplace | subzero |
| transformation | misbehave | submarine |
| transfer | misunderstand | submerge |
| transplant | mistake | subtotal |

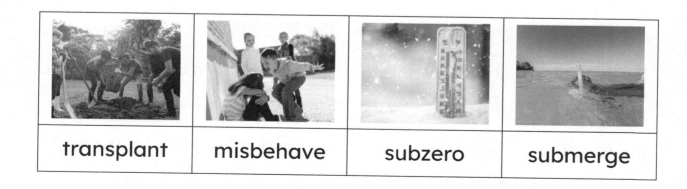

| transplant | misbehave | subzero | submerge |
|---|---|---|---|

# Sentences

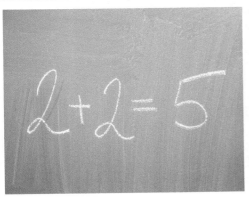  

1. A caterpillar transforms into a butterfly.

2. What is the subtotal? What is the total?

3. I've misplaced my phone. I can't find it.

4. Sorry, that's not correct. I made a mistake.

5. Does your city have good public transportation?

6. You can use your phone to translate words from one language to another language.

# Prefix Opposites in-, ex-, de-

## Opposites

inhale / exhale

interior / exterior

import / export

increase / decrease

inflate / deflate

ascend / descend

withdraw / deposit

income / expense

enter / exit

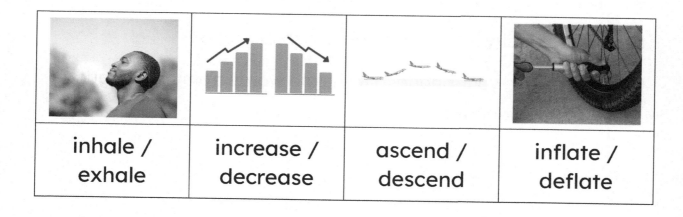

| inhale / exhale | increase / decrease | ascend / descend | inflate / deflate |

## Sentences

1. Germany, Japan, and the United States are the countries that export the most cars.

2. If you have a bank account, you can go to the bank to deposit a check or withdraw cash.

3. Where is the exit? It's over there.

4. If you need to inflate a tire, you can use an air machine at a gas station or a tire shop.

5. You need to report your monthly income to qualify for the program.

6. He is painting the exterior of the house.

# Kangaroos

A kangaroo is a very unique animal. It is a large animal that jumps. Almost all of the kangaroos in the world live in Australia. The kangaroo is a national symbol of Australia, and appears on the Australian one dollar coin.

A female kangaroo has a pouch where she carries her young. A young kangaroo is called a joey. A joey can drink its mother's milk from inside the pouch. A joey will stay in its mother's pouch until it is about six to ten months old. After that, it is ready to be out on its own.

Kangaroos have big feet, strong legs, and a muscular tail. A large kangaroo can hop more than 8 meters (or 26 feet) in a single jump. They can move really fast. Some kangaroos can comfortably hop at a speed of more than 55 kph (or 34 mph).

Kangaroos are herbivores. They eat plants and grass, but no meat. Kangaroos do not need a lot of water to survive. They can go for long periods of time without drinking. Kangaroos are very interesting animals.

# Kiwi Birds

A kiwi is a very unique animal. It is a small bird that can only be found in New Zealand. It is the national symbol of New Zealand, and it appears on the New Zealand one dollar coin.

A kiwi is a bird, but it cannot fly. Instead, it has strong legs and can run quite fast. A kiwi bird has a long beak with nostrils at the end. It has a very good sense of smell. Kiwi birds eat worms and insects, as well as berries and seeds.

A kiwi is approximately the same size as a chicken. It has feathers that look like hair, and it has whiskers like a cat. It doesn't have a tail.

Kiwi are nocturnal. They are most active at night and usually sleep during the day. Kiwi sleep in burrows in the ground.

There used to be millions of kiwi birds in New Zealand, but today, there aren't very many left. Their numbers are declining due to new predators and lost habitat. The people of New Zealand are working hard to protect kiwi.

# Homophones 1

| | |
|---|---|
| meat / meet | where / wear |
| ate / eight | new / knew |

1. Do you like to eat <u>meat</u>?
2. Nice to <u>meet</u> you! Thank you for coming to this <u>meet</u>ing.

3. What did you eat last night? We <u>ate</u> pasta.
4. Five plus three is <u>eight</u>.

5. <u>Where</u> is the office? Over there!
6. When it is cold outside, I <u>wear</u> a jacket and a hat.

7. My friend got a <u>new</u> car. It's really nice.
8. Did you know the answer? Yes, I <u>knew</u> it!

| meat | meet | ate | eight |
|---|---|---|---|

| I / eye | four / for |
| right / write | no / know |

9. <u>I</u> am a student. <u>I</u> go to school. <u>I</u> like my class.

10. Your nose, mouth, ears, and <u>eye</u>s are parts of your face.

11. Should I turn <u>right</u> or left?

12. In school, we learn to read and <u>write</u>.

13. Two plus two is <u>four</u>.

14. This is a gift <u>for</u> you. <u>For</u> me? Yes, <u>for</u> you!

15. He has <u>no</u> money.

16. What is your brother's address? Sorry, I don't <u>know</u>.

| right | write | four | for |

# Homophones 2

| | |
|---|---|
| hi  /  high | way  /  weigh |
| see  /  sea | here  /  hear |

1.  <u>Hi</u>! How are you?

2.  You can turn the heat <u>high</u> or low.


3.  <u>See</u> you tomorrow! OK, I will <u>see</u> you later.

4.  The Black <u>Sea</u> is a big body of water in Europe.


5.  Which <u>way</u>? This <u>way</u> or that <u>way</u>?

6.  How much do you <u>weigh</u>?


7.  Please, come over <u>here</u>.

8.  Can you <u>hear</u> me? Yes, I can <u>hear</u> you.

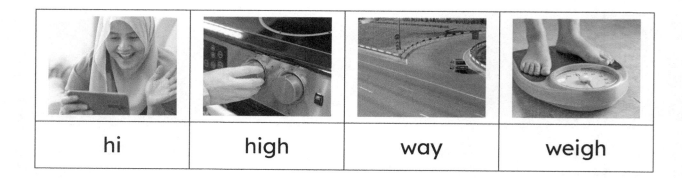

| hi | high | way | weigh |
|---|---|---|---|

one / won      break / brake

flower / flour      to / two / too

9. <u>One</u>, two, three, four, five...

10. Did you win the game? Yes, we <u>won</u>!

11. She likes to smell the <u>flower</u>s.

12. To make bread, you need <u>flour</u>.

13. We take a lunch <u>break</u> from 12:00 to 12:30.

14. A car has a gas pedal and a <u>brake</u> pedal. Use the <u>brake</u> to stop.

15. The kids are going <u>to</u> school. Their mom is going <u>to</u> work.

16. She has <u>two</u> children.

17. How much did it cost? Wow, that's <u>too</u> much!

| flower | flour | break | brake |

# Homophones 3

| | |
|---|---|
| hour  /  our | sell  /  cell |
| week  /  weak | plane  /  plain |

1. There are sixty minutes in one <u>hour</u>.

2. We have lived here for two years. <u>Our</u> house is nice.

3. There are seven days in a <u>week</u>.

4. The opposite of strong is <u>weak</u>.

5. She <u>sell</u>s fruit and vegetables at the farmer's market.

6. How much is your <u>cell</u> phone bill every month?

7. You can buy a <u>plane</u> ticket to visit another country.

8. Do you want the chocolate one or the <u>plain</u> one?

| plane | plain | sell | cell |

70

| | |
|---|---|
| son / sun | threw / through |
| aunt / ant | they're / their / there |

9. They have one daughter and one <u>son</u>.

10. The <u>sun</u> is bright today. I need some <u>sun</u>glasses.

11. My uncle and <u>aunt</u> are coming to visit. They are my father's brother and sister.

12. We have a problem with <u>ant</u>s in our kitchen.

13. He <u>threw</u> the ball to his dad. Now his dad will throw it back.

14. This train goes <u>through</u> a long tunnel.

15. They are cleaning. <u>They're</u> cleaning the kitchen.

16. They have a car. <u>Their</u> car is red.

17. Where should I put this? Put it over <u>there</u>.

| aunt | ant | threw | through |
|------|-----|-------|---------|

# Homophones 4

| wait / weight | road / rode |
|---|---|
| do / due | pair / pear |

1.  Please <u>wait</u>. We will help you soon.

2.  What is your height? What is your <u>weight</u>?


3.  <u>Do</u> you speak English? Yes, I <u>do</u>.

4.  When is your baby <u>due</u>? The baby is <u>due</u> in October.


5.  You can drive on a <u>road</u>.

6.  Did you ride the bus today? Yes, I <u>rode</u> the bus.


7.  I need to get a <u>pair</u> of gloves and a <u>pair</u> of glasses.

8.  A <u>pear</u> is one kind of fruit. I like to eat <u>pear</u>s.

| wait | weight | pair | pear |

mail / male          blue / blew

red / read           by / buy / bye

9.   They will send a letter in the <u>mail</u>.

10.  <u>Male</u> means man. Female means woman.

11.  What color is the jacket? It is a <u>red</u> jacket.

12.  Did you read the book? Yes, I <u>read</u> it.

13.  What color is the shirt? It is a <u>blue</u> shirt.

14.  There was a bad storm yesterday. The wind <u>blew</u> down a big tree.

15.  Where is the cat? The cat is over there, <u>by</u> the door.

16.  Our TV is broken. I want to <u>buy</u> a new TV.

17.  See you later! Good <u>bye</u>!

| blew | by | buy | bye |

# The United Kingdom

The United Kingdom is a country in western Europe. The UK is unique because it consists of four nations that are united together into one country. The four nations are England, Wales, Scotland, and Northern Ireland.

The UK is made up of many islands. The largest island is called Great Britain. The nations of Wales, England, and Scotland are on this island. The second largest island is called Ireland. Only the northern part of Ireland is part of the United Kingdom. The main part of Ireland is a separate independent country.

The most common language spoken in the UK is English. The flag of the United Kingdom is called the Union Jack. Its colors are red, white, and blue. The currency in the United Kingdom is called the pound. The coins and bills feature the image of the queen or king.

A queen or king is the head of the country, but the government is run by the Prime Minister. The Prime Minister and the Parliament are elected by the people of the UK.

# London

The capital city of the United Kingdom is London. London is one of the largest cities in Europe. The population of London is over nine million. It is a very ethnically diverse city. About 30% of people in London were born in other countries. English is the main language, but over 200 other languages are spoken by London residents.

London is located in the southeastern part of England. It is the location of the United Kingdom's government. People who are elected to Parliament meet in London in the Palace of Westminster. The building has a famous clock tower with bells that chime every hour. The biggest bell is nicknamed Big Ben.

London was the first city in the world to have an underground public transportation system. The railway system is called the Tube because some sections go through round underground tunnels. The underground trains started running in 1863. Today, the system has more than 270 stations and a network of track lines that total over 400 kilometers.

# Multiple Meanings 1

### tablet

1. computer          I watch movies on my <u>tablet</u>.
2. medicine       Take one <u>tablet</u> four times a day.

### keep

1. hold; have     Here's some money. You can <u>keep</u> it.
2. continue       Don't stop. <u>Keep</u> going!

### center

1. middle         Try to get it in the <u>center</u> of the circle.
2. place          I have a job at the medical <u>center</u>.

### left

1. past tense of leave   What time did he leave? He <u>left</u> at 3:00.
2. opposite of right    Which way, right or <u>left</u>?
3. remaining        Do you want pizza? There are 3 pieces <u>left</u>.

| tablet | tablet | center | center |

## break

1. to get broken     How did you <u>break</u> your arm? I fell down.
2. relax at work      At 9:00, we take a <u>break</u> for 15 minutes.

## can

1. be able to         <u>Can</u> you help me? Yes, I <u>can</u>.
2. metal container    Do you want fresh corn, or corn in a <u>can</u>?

## shift

1. work time          Do you work the AM <u>shift</u> or PM <u>shift</u>?
2. control a car      You need to <u>shift</u> the car to D to drive.

## check

1. look               The dentist will <u>check</u> your teeth.
2. money              I get a pay<u>check</u> every other Friday.

| 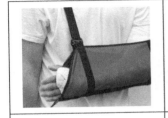 |  |  |  |
|---|---|---|---|
| break | break | can | can |

# Multiple Meanings 2

| fine | |
|---|---|
| 1. good | How are you? <u>Fine</u>, thanks! |
| 2. money | I got a parking ticket. It's a $50 <u>fine</u>. |

| ring | |
|---|---|
| 1. jewelry on finger | She likes to wear <u>ring</u>s on her fingers. |
| 2. phone sound | The phone is <u>ring</u>ing. |

| saw | |
|---|---|
| 1. past tense of see | Did you see her? Yes, I <u>saw</u> her over there. |
| 2. tool that can cut | Where can I buy a <u>saw</u>? |

| date | |
|---|---|
| 1. day on calendar | What is the <u>date</u> today? |
| 2. fruit | Do you like to eat <u>date</u>s? |
| 3. romantic meeting | They are going on a <u>date</u> on Saturday. |

|  |  |  |  |
|---|---|---|---|
| fine | fine | saw | saw |

### trip

1. fall down      Be careful. Don't <u>trip</u>!
2. vacation      We are taking a <u>trip</u> to visit family.

### feet

1. body part      You have two hands and two <u>feet</u>.
2. measurement      1 meter is about the same as 3 <u>feet</u>.

### run

1. move fast on feet      He likes to <u>run</u> for exercise.
2. manage      We vote for people to <u>run</u> the government.

### right

1. opposite of left      Do you hold a pen with your <u>right</u> hand?
2. correct      Can you check this? Is this <u>right</u>?
3. freedom      One <u>right</u> we have is freedom of speech.

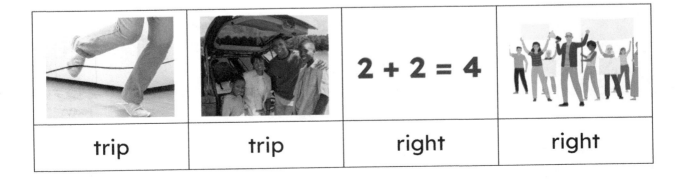

| trip | trip | right | right |

# Multiple Meanings 3

## nail

1. on your finger     I need to cut my finger<u>nail</u>.
2. hammer and nail     Where can I buy a hammer and <u>nail</u>?

## rest

1. relax     After work, I like to sit down and <u>rest</u>.
2. what remains     There's a little more. Do you want the <u>rest</u>?

## light

1. light / dark     You can use a <u>light</u> to see in the dark.
2. light / heavy     Is it heavy? No, it's pretty <u>light</u>.

## point

1. number     We have 3 <u>point</u>s. They have 2 <u>point</u>s.
2. show with finger     <u>Point</u> to your ears.
3. small dot     2.5 is "two <u>point</u> five" or two and a half.

| nail | nail | light | light |

## feel

1. mood or feeling      How do you <u>feel</u>? I <u>feel</u> hot and tired.

2. touch      You can <u>feel</u> your pulse in your neck.

## fly

1. go up in the air      Birds and planes are things that can <u>fly</u>.

2. a bug      I can't sleep. There is a big <u>fly</u> in my room.

## letter

1. alphabet      The English alphabet has 26 <u>letter</u>s.

2. paper      They will send you a <u>letter</u> in the mail.

## kind

1. type      What <u>kind</u> of food do you like?

2. nice      My neighbor is a very <u>kind</u> woman.

| | | African food<br>Mexican food<br>Indian food<br>Chinese food | |
|---|---|---|---|
| **fly** | **fly** | **kind** | **kind** |

# The Rocky Mountains

The Rocky Mountains are the largest mountain range in North America. They are located in the western part of Canada and the United States. The Rocky Mountains contain many high peaks, including some over 4,000 meters (or 14,000 feet) tall.

A large portion of the Rocky Mountains is land that is protected as National Forests or National Parks. It is land that is managed by the U.S. or Canadian government.

Large animals such as deer, elk, moose, bears, and wolves live in this area. There are also mountain lions and mountain goats.

The Rocky Mountain area gets cold and snowy in the winter and can be dry and hot in the summer. Tourism is an important industry in this region. Every year, millions of people visit the Rocky Mountains. They visit for outdoor recreation like hiking, biking, and skiing. Camping and fishing are also popular. The scenery is beautiful, so you can take a lot of nice photos. It's a great place to visit.

# The Sahara Desert

The Sahara Desert is an enormous desert region in northern Africa. The Sahara Desert covers parts of the countries of Egypt, Libya, Algeria, and others. A desert is an area that receives very little rainfall. Some parts of the Sahara Desert receive less than 2.5 centimeters (or 1 inch) of rain per year.

The Sahara Desert can have extremely hot temperatures. In the summer, temperatures above 40 degrees Celsius (or 104 degrees Fahrenheit) are normal. However, desert temperatures can also be cold, especially at night.

Because the land is very dry, there aren't a lot of plants or animals in the Sahara Desert. Camels are important working animals in the desert because they can handle very hot weather and they can go for a few days without drinking. Some wild animals in the desert include gazelles, foxes, and hyenas. There are also snakes, lizards, and birds. The Sahara Desert is a harsh environment, but also a beautiful landscape.

# Greek and Latin Roots 1

| **view**<br>(look) | **port**<br>(carry) | **spect**<br>(see) |
|---|---|---|
| interview | portable | inspection |
| review | transportation | respect |
| preview | import / export | spectator |
| overview | reporter | spectacles |
| view | airport | spectacular |
| viewpoint | support | expect |

| viewpoint | airport | spectator | spectacles |
|---|---|---|---|

## Sentences

1. We will review tomorrow so you can understand it better.

2. This book will give you  an overview of our company.

3. He is a TV reporter. He reports the news to people.

4. You can use a portable charger to charge your phone.

5. They will come to inspect the house. The inspection is on Saturday.

6. He is a good manager. Everyone respects him because he is helpful and nice.

# Greek and Latin Roots 2

| **vis** (see) | **sign** (mark) | **fin** (end) |
|---|---|---|
| visit | sign | finish |
| visible / invisible | assignment | final |
| supervisor | design | finally |
| visor | signal | infinite |
| television | signature | definitely |
| vision | significant | |

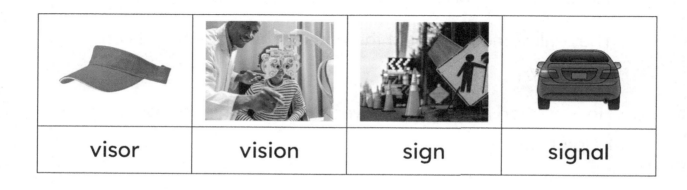

| visor | vision | sign | signal |
|---|---|---|---|

## Sentences

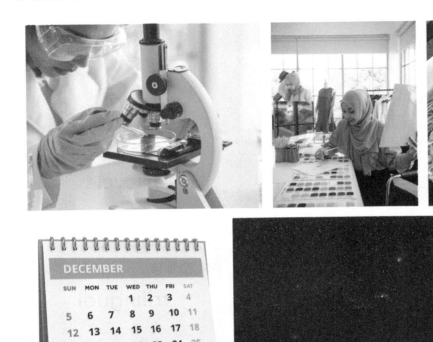

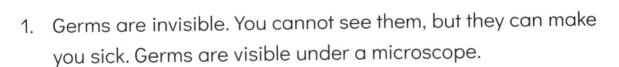

1. Germs are invisible. You cannot see them, but they can make you sick. Germs are visible under a microscope.

2. She designs clothing. She is a fashion designer.

3. Is fish a significant part of your diet?

4. Our final class will be on December 16.

5. How many stars are in the sky? The number is infinite!

6. Can you come? Yes, I can definitely be there.

# Greek and Latin Roots 3

| **uni**<br>(one) | **bi**<br>(two) | **tri**<br>(three) |
|:---:|:---:|:---:|
| unicycle | bicycle | tricycle |
| university | binoculars | triangle |
| uniform | bilingual | trilingual |
| united | biped | triathlon |
| universe | biceps | triplets |
| unique | billion | trillion |

| unicycle | binoculars | tricycle | triplets |
|:---:|:---:|:---:|:---:|

## Sentences

1. She has a uniform for work.

2. There are more than a trillion stars in the universe.

3. He can speak Arabic and English. He is bilingual.

4. There are almost 8 billion people in the world.

5. He has big biceps.

6. That window is shaped like a triangle.

# Greek and Latin Roots 4

**multi**
(many)

multilingual

multinational

multiple

multiplication

multimillionaire

multicultural

pentagon

hexagon

octagon

centimeter

millimeter

kilometer

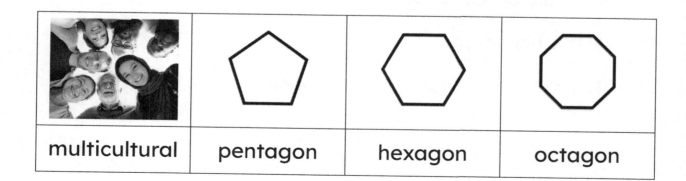

| | | | |
|---|---|---|---|
| multicultural | pentagon | hexagon | octagon |

# Sentences

1. She can speak five languages. She is multilingual.

2. He is a multimillionaire and travels in his own personal helicopter.

3. They learn multiplication in school. For example, 5 x 3 = 15.

4. If you cut a meter into 100 parts, you have a centimeter. A fingernail is about one centimeter wide.

5. If you cut a meter into 1000 parts, you have a millimeter. A credit card is about one millimeter thick.

6. If you repeat a meter 1000 times, you have a kilometer. It takes about ten minutes to walk one kilometer.

# Greek and Latin Roots 5

| **graph**<br>(write) | **therm**<br>(heat) | **photo**<br>(light) |
|---|---|---|
| photograph | thermometer | photograph |
| paragraph | thermos | photographer |
| autograph | thermostat | photography |
| autobiography | hypothermia | photosynthesis |
| geography | geothermal | |
| telegraph | | |

| autograph | geography | thermos | geothermal |

# Sentences

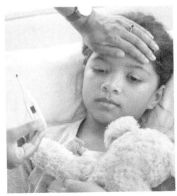
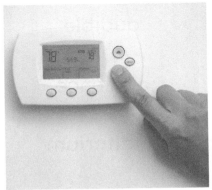

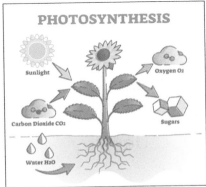

1. A camera takes in light and makes a photograph.

2. Before telephones, you could send a message with a telegraph.

3. You can use a thermometer to check her temperature.

4. You can use the thermostat to control the temperature in your house.

5. She is a professional photographer.

6. Photosynthesis is the way that plants take in light and use it to make energy to grow. You can learn about photosynthesis in a biology class.

# Greek and Latin Roots 6

| **struc** (build) | **dict** (say) | **aud** (listen) |
|---|---|---|
| structure | dictation | audio |
| construction | dictionary | audible |
| destruction | dictator | audience |
| destroy | predict | auditorium |
| instructions | indicate | |
| instructor | | |

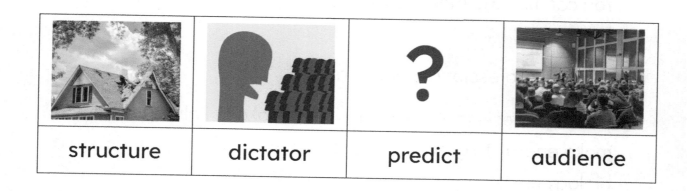

| structure | dictator | predict | audience |
|---|---|---|---|

# Sentences

1. The dog destroyed the pillow.

2. The instructions will tell you how to do it.

3. Dictation is an activity where the teacher says a word or sentence and the students listen and write it.

4. A dictionary is a book that tells you what words mean.

5. You can send a text message or an audio message.

6. Our school has a big auditorium.

# Greek and Latin Roots 7

| **ten**<br>(hold) | **tract**<br>(pull) | **verse**<br>(turn) |
|---|---|---|
| contain | tractor | reverse |
| obtain | traction | anniversary |
| maintain | extract | conversation |
| maintenance | subtraction | diversity |
| tenant | distracted | divorced |
| detention | contract | universe |

| contain | tenant | contract | reverse |
|---|---|---|---|

# Sentences

1. What do you need to do to obtain citizenship in a new country?

2. He has a maintenance job. He fixes things anytime there is a problem.

3. Before you drive in the snow, it's important to get tires with good traction.

4. If you have a bad tooth, the dentist may need to extract it.

5. Next month will be the five year anniversary of the day I came to this country.

6. I like the diversity at our school.

# Greek and Latin Roots 8

| **auto**<br>(self) | **mem**<br>(think) | **mov**<br>(move) |
|---|---|---|
| autobiography | remember | movement |
| automatic | memory | remove |
| automatically | memorize | movie |
| automobile | Memorial Day | automobile |
| auto shop | commemorate | mobile phone |
| auto insurance | memo | immobile |

| automatic | memo | movie | immobile |
|---|---|---|---|

# Sentences

1886

1. The first automobile was invented in 1886.

2. He is an auto mechanic. He works at an auto shop.

3. If you drive a car, you need to have auto insurance.

4. It's a good idea to teach children to memorize their phone number and address. If they get lost, it will help a lot!

5. What are some good memories from your past?

6. They always remove their shoes before they go inside.

# Greek and Latin Roots 9

| **cit** | **rel** | **scrib** |
|:---:|:---:|:---:|
| (people) | (connect) | (write) |
| city | related | scribe |
| citizen | relatives | scribble |
| citizenship | relationship | scripture |
| civil rights | relate | prescription |
| civil war | correlation | transcript |

| city | citizen | scribble | scripture |
|:---:|:---:|:---:|:---:|

# Sentences

| High School Transcript | |
| --- | --- |
| English | 4.0 Credits |
| Math | 3.0 Credits |
| History | 2.0 Credits |
| Science | 2.0 Credits |
| Geography | 1.0 Credits |
| Art | 1.0 Credits |
| Dance | 1.0 Credits |
| P.E. | 1.0 Credits |
| Auto Shop | 1.0 Credits |

1. A civil war is a war between people in the same country.

2. A lot of people have worked hard to fight for civil rights.

3. We are family. We are related.

4. What is your relationship? They are my aunt and uncle.

5. The doctor gave me a prescription.

6. This is a copy of my high school transcript.

# Greek and Latin Roots 10

| **form**<br>(shape) | **lect**<br>(choose) | **part**<br>(part) |
|---|---|---|
| transform | select | apartment |
| transformation | selection | department |
| information | collect | depart |
| performance | collection | partner |
| informal | elect | participate |
| uniform | election | participant |

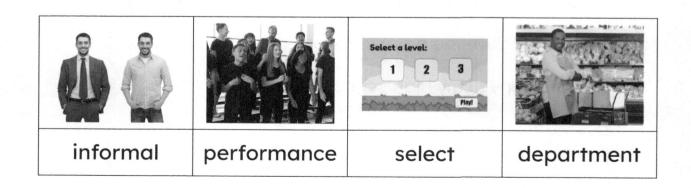

| informal | performance | select | department |
|---|---|---|---|

102

# Sentences

1. We are going to collect money and clothes to send to people that need help.

2. You need to work with a partner to complete this assignment.

3. Do you participate in any sports?

4. How many participants are in this meeting?

5. What time does your flight depart? It departs at 3:30 and arrives at 5:30.

6. In the United States, people elect a new president every four years.

# Accented Syllables

<table>
<tr><td>

apply

application

applicant

</td><td>

certified

certificate

certification

</td></tr>
<tr><td>

nation

national

nationality

</td><td>

resident

residence

residential

</td></tr>
<tr><td>

register

registration

</td><td>

eligible

eligibility

</td></tr>
<tr><td>

photograph

photographer

</td><td>

celebrate

celebration

</td></tr>
</table>

|  |  | 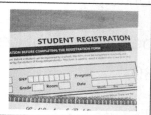 |  |
|---|---|---|---|
| certificate | resident | registration | celebration |

## Sentences

1. I want to apply for a job in the produce department.
   OK, the application is online.
   How many applicants have applied already?

2. She is a Certified Nursing Assistant.
   She got her certificate last year.
   The certification test was not easy.

3. Somalia is a nation in eastern Africa.
   This is the national flag of Somalia.
   My friend is Somalian. What about you? What's your nationality?

4. I would like to register for English classes.
   OK, please fill out this registration form.

5. Some people may be eligible to receive housing assistance.
   Eligibility is based on household income.

# COVID - 19

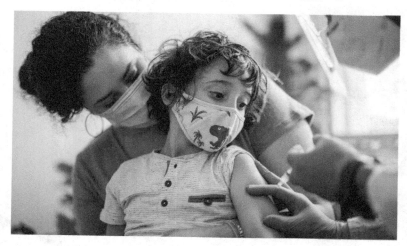

A virus is a type of germ that can make people sick. There are hundreds of different viruses that affect people. For example, the flu and the common cold are both caused by viruses.

In 2019, a new virus appeared. Because the virus was new to humans, many people got sick easily. The virus spread rapidly, and by 2020, it became a worldwide pandemic.

Covid-19 stands for Coronavirus Disease, 2019. Under a microscope, a coronavirus looks like a ball with spiky points. *Corona* means *crown*. The end of each spiky point looks like a crown.

In 2019, Covid-19 was a new disease. It caused serious illness for some people, especially the elderly and people with weak immune systems. With time, people are building more immunity to Covid-19, so it is becoming less dangerous. Vaccines can also help prevent serious illness.

Covid-19 will be around for a long time, just like the flu and the common cold. To help prevent the spread of viruses, you can wash your hands regularly, talk to a doctor about vaccines, and stay home when you are sick.

# Diabetes

Diabetes is a common disease that affects more than 420 million people worldwide. People with diabetes have trouble controlling their blood sugar. If diabetes is not managed carefully, it can lead to other serious long-term complications.

When you eat food, your body breaks it down into glucose, or sugar. Glucose gives you energy. Your body uses an important hormone called insulin to regulate the amount of glucose in your blood. People who have diabetes don't produce enough insulin on their own, so their blood sugar can get too high or too low.

If a person's blood sugar is too high, they may experience symptoms such as frequent urination and increased thirst. If a person's blood sugar is too low, they may experience symptoms such as headaches, shakiness, dizziness, and fatigue.

If you have diabetes, it's important to check your blood sugar levels regularly. You may need medication or insulin injections to help you control your blood sugar. A doctor can help you understand how to manage diabetes with medication, exercise, and healthy food.

# Final Syllables: -al, -el, -le

| total | label | bicycle |
| signal | tunnel | triangle |
| final | level | example |
| personal | towel | vehicle |
| traditional | bagel | trouble |
| additional | squirrel | shuttle |
| mental | shovel | terrible |
| physical | travel | syllable |
| medical | cancel | recycle |

| traditional | bagel | vehicle | shuttle |

# Sentences

1.  Exercise is important for your physical health.

2.  Personal connections are important for your mental health.

3.  A squirrel is a small animal that can climb trees.

4.  You can use the blue bin to recycle paper, plastic, and metal.

5.  We need a shovel to dig a hole so we can plant the tree.

6.  He made some bad choices, and now he is in a lot of trouble.

## Final Syllables: -ture, -sure

| | | |
|---|---|---|
| signature | culture | sure |
| temperature | furniture | pressure |
| picture | nature | insure |
| future | fracture | measure |
| structure | agriculture | pleasure |
| feature | adventure | treasure |

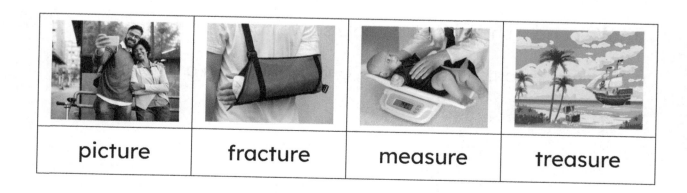

| picture | fracture | measure | treasure |
|---|---|---|---|

## Sentences

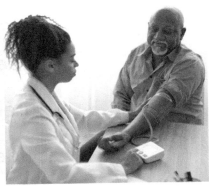

1. A furniture store is a place where you can buy sofas, tables, chairs, and beds.

2. Henna is an important part of my culture.

3. Being outside in nature is good for your mind and your body.

4. Agriculture is a major industry in this area.

5. Can you help me? Sure!

6. The doctor will check your blood pressure.

# Final Syllables: -ent, -ant

| | |
|---|---|
| current | assistant |
| absent | immigrant |
| urgent | tenant |
| frequent | vacant |
| recent | significant |
| resident | brilliant |
| parent | infant |
| accident | participant |
| president | applicant |
| intelligent | instant |
| silent | pregnant |
| excellent | important |

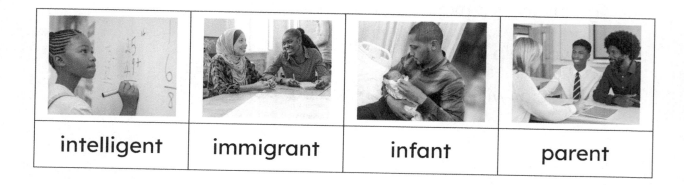

| intelligent | immigrant | infant | parent |
|---|---|---|---|

## Sentences

1.  What is your current job? Do you have any previous jobs?

2.  He is absent today. He has an appointment.

3.  An urgent care center is a place where you can get medical treatment right away. You don't need to wait for an appointment.

4.  We need a copy of your three most recent pay statements.

5.  Right now this building is vacant, but a new business is planning to move in soon.

6.  Instant noodles are ready to eat in three minutes. Instant means quick.

## Final Syllables: -ence, -ance

| | |
|---|---|
| silence | entrance |
| sentence | distance |
| audience | insurance |
| science | performance |
| experience | maintenance |
| difference | appliance |
| conference | balance |
| independence | ambulance |
| residence | attendance |

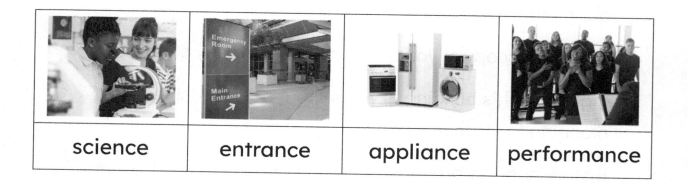

| science | entrance | appliance | performance |
|---|---|---|---|

# Sentences

1. Do you have any experience working in a restaurant?

2. What is the difference between a cold and the flu?

3. We have a parent-teacher conference next week.

4. When you are driving, you need to keep a safe distance between your car and the car in front of you. Don't get too close.

5. If you have a car, you need to insure it. Car insurance protects you and others if you have an accident.

6. Can you balance on one foot for twenty seconds?

# Final Syllables: -ci.., -ti.., -si..

| | | |
|---|---|---|
| social | partial | permission |
| special | initial | transmission |
| official | residential | profession |
| commercial | essential | television |
| financial | potential | decision |

| | |
|---|---|
| delicious | nutritious |
| precious | cautious |
| spacious | ambitious |
| suspicious | infectious |

| | |
|---|---|
| physician | patient |
| musician | caution |
| electrician | action |
| pediatrician | option |

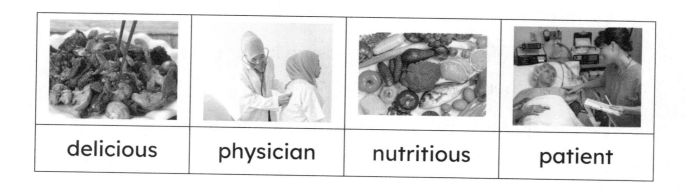

| delicious | physician | nutritious | patient |
|---|---|---|---|

# Sentences

1. This school has special education services for students who need extra help.

2. Liberia is a country in western Africa. There are more than 20 local languages. English is the official government language.

3. Essential means needed. A knife is an essential kitchen tool.

4. You need to be very cautious when you are driving the forklift.

5. You can ask the teacher for permission if you need to leave the room.

6. She is an ambitious student. She works hard and wants to do well. She has a lot of big plans for her future.

# Appendix

## 1. Verbs

A verb is an action word.

Verbs have many forms.

Regular verbs use -ed in the past tense.  Irregular verbs do not.

| Regular Verbs | Irregular Verbs |
|---|---|
| clean<br>cleans<br>cleaning<br>cleaned<br>will clean<br>going to clean | give<br>gives<br>giving<br>gave<br>will give<br>going to give |

## 2. Nouns

A noun is a person, place, or thing.

Nouns can be singular (1), or plural (more than 1).

Regular nouns use -s to make a plural.  Irregular nouns do not.

| Regular Nouns | Irregular Nouns |
|---|---|
| student - students<br>room - rooms<br>pencil - pencils<br>baby - babies | man - men<br>woman - women<br>child - children<br>person - people |

## 3. Contractions

A contraction is two small words that are combined with an apostrophe.

| | | | | |
|---|---|---|---|---|
| I'm | isn't | can't | I'll | I've |
| he's | aren't | won't | he'll | they've |
| she's | wasn't | couldn't | she'll | could've |
| you're | weren't | shouldn't | they'll | should've |
| they're | don't | wouldn't | I'd | would've |
| we're | doesn't | haven't | he'd | what's |
| it's | didn't | hasn't | she'd | where's |

## 4. Apostrophe + s

When you add apostrophe + s after a noun, it means "of" or "belongs to."

| | |
|---|---|
| the teacher's phone | (the phone of the teacher) |
| the manager's office | (the office of the manager) |
| Sam's laptop | (the laptop that belongs to Sam) |
| Alisha's car | (the car that belongs to Alisha) |
| Jessica's bag | (the bag that belongs to Jessica) |

## 5. Suffixes

A suffix is a word part at the <u>end</u> of a word.

| -y | -ly | -less | -ful | -able |
|---|---|---|---|---|
| dirty | slowly | painless | helpful | breakable |
| sleepy | safely | wireless | colorful | available |
| rainy | quietly | jobless | stressful | washable |

| -er | -or | -ist | -ment | -ness |
|---|---|---|---|---|
| painter | instructor | pharmacist | apartment | happiness |
| teacher | director | artist | appointment | sadness |
| baker | doctor | dentist | basement | illness |

## 6. Prefixes

A prefix is a word part at the <u>beginning</u> of a word.

| un- | re- | dis- | in- | pre- |
|---|---|---|---|---|
| unhappy | reheat | disagree | inexpensive | preschool |
| uncooked | refill | disconnect | incorrect | pretest |
| untied | reset | disappear | incomplete | precooked |

| inter- | super- | trans- | mis- | sub- |
|---|---|---|---|---|
| interview | supervisor | translation | misspell | subway |
| international | supermarket | transportation | misplace | subzero |
| intersection | superintendent | transfer | mistake | subtotal |

# 7. Homophones

Homophones are two words that have the same sound, but different spelling and different meaning.

| | | |
|---|---|---|
| meat / meet<br>ate / eight<br>where / wear<br>new / knew | I / eye<br>right / write<br>four / for<br>no / know | hi / high<br>see / sea<br>way / weigh<br>here / hear |

# 8. Multiple Meanings

Some words in English have more than one meaning.

| tablet | |
|---|---|
| 1. computer | I watch movies on my <u>tablet</u>. |
| 2. medicine | Take one <u>tablet</u> four times a day. |

| keep | |
|---|---|
| 1. hold; have | Here's some money. You can <u>keep</u> it. |
| 2. continue | Don't stop. <u>Keep</u> going! |

| center | |
|---|---|
| 1. middle | Try to get it in the <u>center</u> of the circle. |
| 2. place | I have a job at the medical <u>center</u>. |

## 9. Greek and Latin Roots

Greek and Latin roots can help you figure out many words in English.

| view | port | spect | vis | sign |
|------|------|-------|-----|------|
| interview | import | inspection | visit | assignment |
| review | export | respect | visible | design |
| preview | airport | expect | vision | signal |
| **fin** | **uni, bi, tri** | **therm** | **mem** | **mov** |
| finish | unicycle | thermometer | memory | remove |
| final | bicycle | thermostat | memorize | movie |
| definitely | tricycle | hypothermia | remember | immobile |

## 10. Final Syllables

These are some common final syllables in English:

| -al | -el | -le | -ture | -sure |
|-----|-----|-----|-------|-------|
| medical | label | bicycle | signature | sure |
| physical | tunnel | triangle | temperature | pressure |
| emotional | level | example | picture | measure |
| **-ent / -ant** | **-ence / -ance** | **-ci..** | **-ti..** | **-si..** |
| resident | silence | social | residential | permission |
| parent | difference | delicious | nutritious | television |
| assistant | entrance | physician | patient | decision |

# 11. Academic Vocabulary

Academic vocabulary is common in informational text, and may be less common in spoken conversation.

**active**: moving around; 65

**affect**: cause something to change; 106, 107

**amount**: number; 107

**appear**: can be seen; 64, 65, 106

**approximately**: about; around; almost; 65

**area**: place; 82, 83

**as well as**: and also; 65

**avoid**: stay away; 53

**beautiful**: very nice looking; 82

**break it down**: break it into smaller parts; 107

**bright**: giving off a lot of light; 43

**building**: 1. (n) structure; 2. (v) making; 106

**carry**: take; 64

**caused by**: happens because of; 106

**center**: 1. middle, 2. place; 52

**chime**: make noise (like a bell); 75

**circulate**: go around in a circle; 53

**coins and bills**: types of money; 74

**comfortably**: easily; 64

**common**: happens a lot; 74, 107

**complication**: problem; 107

**connected**: linked together; 52

**connection**: link between things; 52

**consist**: include; 74

**contain**: have inside; 82

**control**: manage; supervise; 52

**covered**: all over; all around; 42, 83

**currency**: money; 74

**declining**: going down; 65

**diverse**: different; 75

**dry**: no water; opposite of wet; 43, 82, 83

**due to**: because of; 65

**dusty**: has dust on it; 43

**easier**: more easy; 52

**easily**: in an easy way; 106

**elect**: vote; 74

**enormous**: very big; 83

**enough**: as much as you need; 42, 107

**environment**: place; land; 83

**especially**: mostly; even more; 83, 106

**ethnically**: culturally; 75

**experience**: 1. (n) skill; 2. (v) feel; 107

**extreme**: more than normal; 43

**extremely**: very, very; 83

**facing**: looking at; 42

**famous**: well known; 75

**fatigue**: tiredness; 107

**feature**: show; 74

**feel**: 1. experience emotion; 2. touch; 53

**female**: woman; 64

**for example**: such as; like; 52

**forest**: a place with a lot of trees; 82

**frequent**: happening a lot; 107

**giant**: very, very big; 42

**habitat**: the place where an animal lives; 65

**handle**: 1. use to open a door; 2. deal with; 83

**harsh**: difficult; 83

**however**: but; 42, 43

**human**: person; 106

**image**: picture; 74

**including**: having in the group; 82

**increase**: happen more; 107

**independent**: free; not controlled by anyone; 74

**industry**: business; 82

**injection**: shot; 107

**injury**: hurt; 52

**instead**: in place of; 65

**interesting**: holding attention; 64

**is called**: is named; 42

**keep**: 1. hold; 2. continue; 52

**landscape**: the land you can see; 83

**largest**: most large; 82

**lead to**: go to; 107

**located**: placed; 52, 53, 82

**movement**: the act of moving; 52

**nation**: country; 74

**national**: of the country; 64, 65

**network**: group of connected things; 52, 75

**nickname**: friendly name; 75

**nocturnal**: active at night; 65

**occur**: happen; 43

**on its own**: without help; 64, 107

**peak**: the top point of a mountain; 82

**percent**: out of 100; 75

**period**: a length of time; 64

**popular**: a lot of people like it; 82

**population**: number of people; 75

**portion**: part; 82

**pouch**: pocket; 64

**prevent**: stop; 106

**produce**: make; 107

**protect**: keep safe; 43, 65, 82

**public**: for everyone; 75

**railway**: train; 75

**range**: area; 82

**rapidly**: fast; quickly; 106

**receive**: get; 83

**reflect**: show it back; 43

**region**: place; area; 82

**regularly**: often; a lot of times; 106, 107

**regulate**: control; 107

**resident**: person living in a place; 75

**revolve**: go around; 42

**rotate**: turn; 42

**round**: like a circle; 43, 75

**run**: 1. move fast on your feet; 2. manage; 74

**scenery**: what you see outside; 82

**section**: part; 75

**separate**: not together; 74

**serious**: big; important; 106, 107

**shine**: give light; 42, 43

**signal**: message; 52

**single**: one; 64

**speed**: fast or slow; 64

**sphere**: a shape like a ball; 42

**spiky**: like a sharp spike; 106

**spread**: move from the center out; 106

**stands for**: is a short way to write; 106

**such as**: for example; 82, 107

**support**: hold up; help; 42

**surface**: top; 42, 43

**survive**: continue to live; 64

**symbol**: a sign to represent something; 64, 65

**system**: a group of things working together; 75

**the rest of**: the others; 53

**thin**: skinny; 43

**through**: in, out; 75

**throughout**: all over; everywhere; 52

**total**: all of it together; 75

**tourism**: people visiting; 82

**tower**: a very tall building; 75

**tunnel**: a way underground; 75

**type**: example; 53, 106

**unique**: different; 42, 64, 65, 74

**united**: together; 74

**until**: up to; 64

**used to**: in the past; 65

**visible**: can be seen; 43

**wear**: put on the body; 43, 52

**worldwide**: all over the world; 106

# Certificate of Achievement

awarded to

for successfully completing

## abc English Phonics Level 4

Teacher Signature

Date

Made in the USA
Las Vegas, NV
09 October 2024

96556899R00072